Jazz After Dinner

Jazz After Dinner

Selected Poems

Leonard A. Slade Jr.

State University of New York Press

Published by
State University of New York Press, Albany

© 2006 State University of New York

For information, contact State University of New York Press, Albany, NY
www.sunypress.edu

Production by Kelli Williams
Marketing by Fran Keneston

Library of Congress Cataloging-in-Publication Data

Slade, Leonard A.
 Jazz after dinner : selected poems / Leonard A. Slade, Jr.
  p. cm.
 ISBN-13: 978-0-7914-6947-7 (hardcover : alk. paper)
 ISBN-10: 0-7914-6947-6 (hardcover : alk. paper)
 ISBN-13: 978-0-7914-6948-4 (pbk : alk. paper)
 ISBN-10: 0-7914-6948-4 (pbk : alk. paper)
 I. Title.

PS3569.L235J39   2006
811'.54–dc22

2006002298

10 9 8 7 6 5 4 3 2 1

For Roberta Hall Slade

———————

Contents

Reasons for Celebration

For My Forefathers

Acknowledgments

Many thanks to the following publications in which the following poems were first published: *Essence Magazine* ("For Our Mothers"), *River City Review* ("Acquaintances"), *The Kentucky Poetry Review* ("The Black Madonna"; "A Child's Play"; "Embden Pond"; "The Street Man"), *The Zora Neale Hurston Forum* ("The Country Preacher's Folk Prayer"; "Plea for Peace"), *The Black Scholar* ("The Anniversary"), *The Griot* ("And Want No More").

Jazz After Dinner

Jazz After Dinner

On a snowy evening I shall feel his sounds,
Quietly moaning, inviting cold air to listen,
Call pleasure from golden keys. Old friends
Will kiss their company, sit to relax and dream.
And music, crying, like an elderly man
That sometimes after sunrise greets morning
Will pervade the world, profusely fill
That evening and me, celebrating life.

For Our Mothers

For our mothers
Born of humble ancestral origins,
Suffering bondage and
Enduring the shackles of slavery
And nurturing a people and a
Country with power and strength
And glory and greatness;

For our mothers,
Queens of the universe
Who give us beauty
And sweetness and light
Radiating with positive energy
And spiritual illumination
And making us rise to all
Propitious occasions wherever
They may be in the world;

For our mothers
Whose gifts to America were
Phillis Wheatley and Frances Harper,
Elizabeth Keckley and Zora Neale Hurston
And Margaret Walker and Gwendolyn Brooks
And Alice Walker and Lorraine Hansberry
And Maya Angelou and Nikki Giovanni;

For our mothers who also shared
Mary McLeod Bethune and Dorothy Height,
Patricia Harris and Barbara Jordan,
Mary Berry and Ruth Simmons
And Toni Morrison and Gloria Naylor
And Rosa Parks and Coretta Scott King
And Oprah Winfrey and Suzan-Lori Parks;

For our mothers walking with faith spreading
Joy, sleeping with tears from painful years,
Shouting when unhappy, praying when the world seemed
Hopeless, trying always to be architects for a better
World, one that will heal all the people
All the sons and daughters and their many generations;

For our mothers
Pillars of the community
And Saviors of the world
Who love us.

Drinking

is a sobering experience
   like sipping vodka in a
topless bar
      multiplying movements
      till flesh burns.

Like one body becoming two
   as problems diminish
      or destroy.

It is beer and wine
   that build fire
for stomachs and fools
      like a wife and child
      scolding for prevention

because alcohol retains
      false power to conquer
      with empty words. It

is like the lion
      drinking blood
      from animals' guts

it is guzzling constantly:
sipping and quenching.

Its wetness is tears;
        camouflaging scars,
            breaking the heart.

It's drowning hopes
        confusion visiting; it's
            drunken sleep and scattered

dreams transforming the now.

We Must Remember

Year after
   year my
      friends remember King
         for his causes—

freedom and justice
   love, hope, and change
      needed now
         Communion and Prayer;

come, King!
   Heaven! Send him,
      his spirit
         to the bowels of the earth

to cleanse,
   coercing racists
      to vomit their evil
         from the past and present

purify souls, renew the earth
   we must remember King,
      police dogs, cold blood,
         black children bombed,

The Mississippi Burning,
  and how bullets
    find apostles and presidents
    and kings;

we must remember
  Montgomery and Memphis,
    the beginning and end,

we must remember
  we must remember
    we must remember
    The Dream.

His Professor

His hair silk
from rich years
his teachings,
quiet words, I observed:

his slow walk, his
humped shoulders and
head bowed;
his breath, short

The books grasped
as if gold
under his arms
resting on yellow notes

published articles,
poems, rhythm;
performing symbols
pupils learn

his labors and
whispers
almost
gone.

My Friend, My Survivor

My friend, my survivor,
    I call you over the telephone,
Anxious and curious and concerned,
    And whom my mind admires.

Sweet life, brave friend, my philosopher
    of immortality,
Your tears and pain document
    our eventual decay.

We sixty-two and sixty-one,
    who love living and learning,
Find eternity in our friendship
    And start to live again.

Overcharged

Overcharged motel, I would not pay,
The beautiful blonde had been okay

Until she charged four nights, not three
And argued unjustly more money against me.

My high blood pressure admittedly rose
As my high voice lost control

For her refusing to admit a wrong
Provoking me to be her super Kahn.

She declined to listen to dramatic oration
And to respect my logic and explanation.

Furious now, I asked the manager
Who for some reason was the motel janitor

To review my bills for accuracy and all
And to take my number for a telephone call.

Overcharging me, a University Professor
Taking on this a dangerous oppressor.

Again my blood pressure unfortunately rose
As the manager like ice almost froze.

She couldn't understand me a mean black
Standing up to defend a simple fact.

Justice and freedom I do need
In this land known for greed.

Sometimes I wish I were President
To avoid dealing with devilment.

Thanksgiving Celebration

The grand hotel by the ocean
houses throngs on Thanksgiving
when scrumptious food is served
and rain pours all day.

It's the best of all times
when children run through the place
and grandparents kiss their offspring,
proud of their seeds,
gracious in their old age,
and happy to
refurbish their minds
and renew their bodies
for the few vacations to follow.

In Praise of Summer

We suffered heat, months, without coolness.
Then, this evening, thunder rolled across the sky:

cool rain began to pour,
bathing the whole state.

Flowers stood at attention,
grass got greener within days.

Now, three days later, birds resume singing
and I begin writing.

Sounds

I still hear the sounds of slaves
   crying on ships
I hear the master's whip cutting black flesh
   for obedience in the hot cotton fields;
I hear John Brown planning a rebellion
   at Harper's Ferry;
I hear Nat Turner's shots killing white
   Americans in West Virginia;
I hear Henry David Thoreau protesting
   slavery and refusing to pay his taxes;
I hear Abraham Lincoln groaning from a
   gunshot to the head at the Ford Theatre;
I hear Harriet Tubman and Sojourner Truth
   running to church to celebrate freedom;
I hear Martin Luther King, Jr., speaking,
   "I'm free at last, I'm free at last.
   Thank God Almighty, I'm free at last."

This My Father

I have visited
my 86-year-old father
at home
in North Carolina

and observed
he was feisty
raising
his voice

Forgive him
he was ill
so afraid
and so alone

Queen for Patrons

I went to the copy center in Albany,
And asked for help from a precious friend,
One with sparkling eyes,
And long black hair kissing her back.
She was the queen for patrons,
Her smiles more radiant than the sun,
Her gentleness of manner sweeter than sugar.
I admired, I observed, I walked away.
My shyness created poetry for her heart,
My words found love for her soul.
She is my poem to keep.

Freedom

Taste of freedom,
Do not abandon me now:

I see men incarcerated
Still in larger numbers.

I see DNA tests
Exonerating many of them.

Taste of freedom,
Bless me now.

He

He was born for us.
He lived for us.
He died for us.
He arose for us.
He ascended the Heavens for us.
He will come again for us.

Hallelujah!
Hallelujah!
Hallelujah!

Citizens in Heaven

He was born for us and for our salvation.
(He came to life in a stable.)

He was the son of a carpenter.
(He lived in a small town.)

He taught us how to pray.
(His language was simple and pure.)

He spread the Word of God.
(The devil and his enemies tried to destroy Him.)

He was crucified on the Cross.
(He died for our sins.)

He rose from the dead and ascended into Heaven.
(We, too, shall one day be citizens in Heaven.)

How Beautiful, O God

How beautiful are the clouds,
   I thank you, God, for the gift of sight.
How beautiful is the earth,
   I thank you for the gift of feeling.
How beautiful are the birds in the morning,
   I thank you for the gift of joy.
How beautiful are the new born babes,
   I thank you for the gift of life.
How beautiful is Your Divine presence,
   I thank you for the promise of eternity.

And When I Die

I want a clean black suit,
A white shirt adorned with
A red necktie and cuff links,
A clean pair of black socks to
Keep my feet warm with shiny
Black shoes serving as my mirror
As I lie stretched out in this
Satin casket being confident about
My good-looking appearance
And still demanding that I get respect.
I want the family to cry their eyeballs out
With my enemies shouting with guilt
Until their wigs get lost going to Heaven.
I want the whole church to holler:
"Please don't go! Please don't go!
Boo-hoo! Boo-hoo!
Please don't go!
Please don't go!"

I Am a Black Man

I am a Black man
my history written with blood
some sweet songs of sorrow
are composed for my soul
and I
can be seen plowing in the fields
Can be heard
humming
in the night

I saw my grandfather coming to America
and I reached back in time
to help him settle in North Carolina
Leaving England forever

and heard his children cry
for freedom with his last
dime . . . he

gave his African queen twelve seeds
of promise planted deep before
slavery ended . . . and I

promised him honor and freedom
I am a Black man
proud as a Lombardy poplar
stronger than granddaddy's roots
defying place
and time
and history
   crucified
      alive
         immortal
Look
  at me and be
healed

Be Grateful

For good health and great hope,
For a loving family and genuine friends,
For the warmth of home,
For the laughter of children,
For the House of Prayer,
For minds to think,
For hearts to love,
For freedom to agree,
For freedom to disagree,
For sunshine and rain,
For harvest and grain,
For the gift of His life,
For the taste of His blood,
For the power of His love,
Be grateful
This Holiday Season.

New Year

I resolve
To eat right
To walk more
To laugh often
To serve well
To forgive mistakes
To love deeply
To read widely
To slow down
To fight racism
To teach hard
To go forward
To be happy.

Advice I Wish I Had Taken Earlier in Life

———————

Expect pain when growing, be
strong, kind and sensitive without
signs of weakness demonstrated.
Be brave in taking risks that stretch
the mind, build the heart, and
nurture the soul;
forgive yourself of past mistakes
with hope, dreams, intercepted light;
cultivate roses in the sun,
below the moon…listen to your
inner voice.
Believe in someone, not too much.
Walk briskly.
Be happy when the clouds burst,
Run in the rain, be
intimate with the universe.
Be beautiful.
Don't forget to fly.

Never Forget

A wedding march,
A child's smile,
A mother's tears,
A good health report,
An excellent teacher,
A sound education,
An American soldier,
A homeless person,
A hungry child,
A loved one's birthday,
A parent's love,
A helping hand,
An inspiring book,
A bird's music,
A funeral song.

The Sad Adult

O Past, stay behind him,
The night once cried,
The fighting physical
Between husband and wife.

Has the heart healed
From the childhood years;
And the dark secret
Buried now risen from the grave?

Be Like the Flower

Be like the flower, which
Blossoming on dark days
Stands erect with pride
Withstands the heavy rain
Yet opens
Knowing it has beauty.

Conversation

Strong language is words,
Flying across the dinner table.
It is feeling.

The debate is mean,
The ego is fragile,
The heart is sad.

That sirloin steak,
That glass of wine—
They saved us all.

That political opinion,
That polemical idea,
Is what makes us strong.

The debate is mean,
The heart is sad.

Black Philosophy

An old field
with pearls priceless
copied for centuries
writ revisionism,

Has kept man strong
rooted in hi(story)
called common sense
culled correctly.

Gems of thought
and the love of wisdom
make man precious
make man free.

Reasons for Celebration

Classic Shed

———————

Tell me is there anyplace quieter,
    Anyplace more bucolic
Than the forest where you rest
    From the bustle of the city?

Are not the sights of bluejays magic,
Are not the sounds of robins musical,
Filling the heart with poetry for pleasure?

Brown Portrait

A young brown woman
in classy clothes

Her walk stately
in the bread store

The worker ignoring
her presence

Her money ready to spend. Looking
intently at the waitress

She requests bountiful bread
to take with her

The hunger for respect satisfied.

Reasons for Celebration

His birth was humble,
His teachings are fire,
His children are followers,
His presence is powerful,
His name is precious,
His love is divine,
His home is eternal.

The Great Mother

Among family
and friends
I like
the mother
strong
children disciplined
father wise
and dogs
running through
the living room
free

As a Friend

See
me in your dreams,
the way I see you
holding
my hand. Late evening
the moon glows, so we walk
slowly, without
words
uttered. (Private
thoughts tonight, nothing
but strolls. What
you are, will have
permanence, or
beginnings. That you
love me, where
you stand, where we embrace
without sounds,
affects the stars,
kisses the moon.)

New York City

I shall always love you,
Your tall and majestic buildings.

I'll cherish your bright
Lights gleaming the whole city.

Some that love you worship you
And commute to absorb your culture,
To sing and dance on Broadway,
Praising old dreams that were shattered
In the World Trade Center resurrected from the dead.

Life and Death

Youth and old age pass
Before we learn the meaning of time.
Our innocence loses itself—
The struggles we overcome
With tears of work and of sacrifice.

The terrible wrongs, the stupid hatred . . .
And still sometimes the moments of love
Remind us of the definitions
That challenge the years.
And what miraculous redemption!

Golden Years

So much have I seen in fifty-eight years,
So much in fifty-eight long years! I can
Remember the first time I kissed my sixteen-year-old
Sweetheart and how her eyes sparkled in the night.
I can remember the special days of long hot summers
When strawberries ripened with sweet juice;
When plums were perfect for picking
And yellow roses blossomed in the frontyard;
Yes, I still remember the five-room house
Where nine children were reared for college.

What painful days they were
When teachers whipped to discipline
And yelled when students did not study!
What days they were when the mule pulled
Heavy plows in the fields to cultivate soil
So that the growth of crops could quicken
During those weeks when school was missed
And studying longer hours to catch up
Inspired determination for all to succeed
When we were taught by teachers and preachers
To be somebody special in the world.

What times we had growing and becoming
And applying our parents' wisdom
And knowledge to cruel living,
Forgiving enemies bent on destroying
The good we were taught;
So much have I learned in fifty-eight years;
I have cherished the sacred moments,
Morning and evening when innocence became experience
I have been so grateful and so happy.

Family-Glorious

family remembrances are forever
if you love
you always remember living at home
with your mom and dad
and if you become weary
after you get grown
then you think about how your
brothers and sisters were
to have glory days during your youth
when you opened your gifts at Christmas
and when you went to church to sing and pray
and your mom cooked soul food
and your dad shared his wisdom about his life
we really appreciate the simple pleasures
when we get together with laughter
at family reunions
and go down memory lane
to celebrate our gifts
our pain that showers our pleasures
our good health
and our parents' harvest
their children and children's children
it really is special when
we show love in little ways

because wealthy love
depends on healthy love
that helps us achieve big things
and I really hope every person
has cause to celebrate family
because we must understand
togetherness is love and living
the Word with family
can keep us quite happy.

How Great You Are

You made the cradle of the earth.
You made clouds for the Heavens.
You made the high hills
and the low valleys.
You assigned the moon for the seasons.
You gave knowledge to the sun.
You made darkness into light.
You laid the foundation of the world.
You gave us Africa and Asia.
North America and South America.
You shared the entire universe.
You caused grass to grow.
You brought food out of the earth.
You traveled the mighty oceans.
You stilled the raging seas.
You dwell in all generations.
You are clothed with honor
and wrapped with majesty and rich in love.
You are our everlasting God.

30 June 1995
Nassau, Bahamas

When I Heard from the Tax Man

When I read the auditor's letter,
I squirmed at an invitation to be his guest,
After I had spent a $6,000 tax refund,
How soon I became ill,
Until the audit was over,
I piled three boxes of evidence on his desk,
In a plush office tower suite.
Examining tons of receipts he concluded,
That Uncle Sam owed me an additional $2,000 refund.
I thanked him for his modern math,
Praised his judgment and meticulosity,
and kissed his invitation goodbye.

Lilacs in Spring

He sucked a thumb in Kentucky,
where his father chopped wood
for warm evenings
in December. He wore old
clothes and walked barefoot
among lilacs in spring. And everywhere
he moved, Indiana and Illinois,
laughter filled the air

as young boys teased his height
and demeaned his clothes. No
child ever praised him,
and he for his suffering honored
her, all children thought small
of his future, except her
who read her *Bible* and loved him
as no other person could.

He studied by candlelight,
savoring words and defining dreams
for America. He was hungry for truth
and debated the pros and cons
of slavery. He promised a united country
but blood would taint freedom.
Brother against brother
sister against sister

blacks against whites
Northerners against Southerners—
they all fought for their cause.
Our father of freedom
bathed America with hope
and then was bathed himself
in cold blood.
Children cried.

Rapping My Way
Home from an English
Conference at Hunter College
On March 22, 1997

Coming from Albany on a rocky train
Made me want to do a special thang.
I arrived at Hunter tired and mean
But the conference today made me clean.
Books and lectures and a million dollar smile
Taught me to stop for just a little while.
Thinking and rapping and hungry for a song
I deduced after meeting that I am the bomb.
Thank you, Hunter, for your mad skills,
You're the best; let's make a deal.
Come to Albany and you will learn
One love from me it'll be my turn.

> Chill out!
> Peace out!
> You're my heart!

What is a Father?

He gives us gifts.
He is a marriage partner.
He is a kind friend.
He is a spiritual giant.

He is a pillar in the community,
Is an architect and dreamer,
Skilled in giving and sharing,
His presence is the wealth of the world.

He is a medicine man and gentle man,
Absorbing pain and curing the blues.
He loves people, His God, and the universe,
Is a warrior defying the years.

May he work for all the stars.
    May he work an eternal moon.

The Black Madonna
(for Elizabeth Langford Slade)

---

picking cotton on
a cold day blisters
decorated her black fingers
in the fields

She crawled on her knees
until the sun bowed
to her. Eight children
planted beneath the stars
The earth felt good to her.

You can see her now
a parched face and folded hands
she kneels in a different place
drinking blood and eating bread
at the altar

Comforted white gloves feel good to her
waving to touch the sky
hymns fill the air
They feel good to her
they feel good to her

A Child's Play

There is a backyard
surrounded
with fences

of different sorts
in a city
on a hill

where a girl
jumps
rope and

inhales air
for a song
circling herself

she hops
on blades
of grass

dying in her
steps; she
ascends her height

the sky
her limit
her joy

For My Forefathers

Black and Beautiful

I am African-American,
Poet of my people,
Black and beautiful,
Sweeter than chocolate candy
Lover of my queen,
Father of my child,
Conscious of my heritage,
Feet tired and hurting,
Heart heavy and hungry,
Attacked because I'm African,
Rejected because I'm Black,
Despised because I'm proud.
But I smile.
I am Black.
I am beautiful.
I am bad.
Just look at me.

Black Woman

Strong woman, black woman
clothed in love, exuding beauty!
I share your darkness,
the sun in your eyes,
The brilliance of your mind,
the lyric in your mouth,
the roots of your soul
And discover myself.

For My Forefathers

For my forefathers
Whipped from Africa
Where children cried
but ships sailed on
And plantation owners were animals
their roars echoing three-hundred years.

For my forefathers
Whose fingers pierced cotton bolls
Beneath the sun roasting human flesh
And darkness told master
to rape black women
for labor and profit.

For my forefathers
Whose masters cursed the North
And justified the South
And debated Lincoln vs. Douglass
And cited slaves in the Bible
And returned to Africa for more.
For my forefathers
Who couldn't read or write
But heard freedom ringing
After Lincoln's Emancipation Proclamation
That taught me to watch
And pray for a new day.

For my forefathers
who loved me.

Family

My family is strong.
They build churches and kneel to pray.
They work through school earning degrees.
They touch property and money grows.
They are architects and dreamers.
My family is strong.

My family is warm and shares
Biscuits and gravy and sweet potato pie,
And hamhocks soaking collard greens,
And white sheets and heavy quilts.
They have many sweet words for Grace.
My family is strong.

Before the Death of Dad

Before maggots suck your marble eyes,
before bones yield to a hollow earth, inviting
black meat to heat cold blood,

I will tell you of the dark days of youth,
of the tears soaking white pillows, of your
hollers inflicting severe pain. I still

love you, the eldest child from your fruitful
penis, your lost sheep destined to lead; I
touch you in your white casket, when I,

nearly 40, still hunger for your laughter
and ache for honeyed words. Open your eyes
in church, hear the voice of your son:

"Plant me again in my mother's womb."

And Want No More

To see her in bed
  is to know
    the meaning of pain.

It's to understand a surgeon's
  scalpel and why.
    How I wish,

desiring her luscious breast, its
  nipple now gone with cancerous
    tissue, my kissing it before, teaching

me. Beauty is something deeper
  that she is a person
    that love tests.

How I loved the breast that
  nurtured my child,
    its milk dripped on pillows

I have sinned,
  worshipping selfish needs,

a honey-brown breast, now
  soaking in blood,
    is like testicles removed.

How humble I am,
   one breast left
      giving us more love, the same

To see a wife's breast disfigured,
   cancerous cells gone
      is to know wellness

and its shared meaning
   is to prolong life
and want no more.

Growing with Grace

You joined me in the Green Mountains
of Bennington, Vermont,
resting in a cottage by the road. I

flirted with your eyes, entered
your mind and body to celebrate
the ups and downs of the years. I

was more than your lover that night
when you whispered gentle words
and sipped champagne. I

was your friend, discovering
sweet ways to love the new years,
growing older with grace.

A Plea for Peace

Let the hawk roost near
the dove
and their eyes
be mirrors, bright and shining, slow
to shut, quick to trust,
sleepless.
—lifting olive branches to travel
the sky and the land.
Silent (No message
but peace) Fly!

Love Should Grow, Not Wither

Love should be silent and whisper
As the gentle wind

Kisses
Cracked cheeks in dead winter,

Fast as the rolling thunder
Lighting the sky before stars dream—

Love should be earthy
As the laughter of children.

Love should build words in time
As the sun rises,

Leaving, as the sun sets
Rays to bloom roses,

Leaving, as the sun hides behind the mountain
Darkness that somehow yields to light—

Love should build words in time
As birds sing and fly.

Love should be free to—
Well.

For all the pain
A heart endures and a salty tear.

For love
The aching sounds and sweet breaths of life—

Love should grow,
not wither.

The Street Man

In New York City I saw a ragged man limp
Around Rockefeller Plaza.
I sat admiring red roses.
He hunted soda cans and crumbs
In trash barrels to feed garbage bags.
Curious,
I watched him depart,
The American Flag waving.

Acquaintances

I meet an acquaintance
whose greeting is icy.
Good evening. I am this,
I am that.
And how about you?
I am me.
My desire to explore her heart and soul
through Antarctica is boundless.
The ice melts.
There is no past.
Here we are,
discovering each other's worlds.
Another continent comes between us:
my mahogany skin, her ivory face,
my woolly hair, her lips of wine
create barriers between us as we go.

Noiseless and impatient, we move to darker
regions of the soul.
Words. Now she has them. She wants more.

Rain

_____

The rain kisses
a cold tin roof.

It tinkles making
music and magic
as mother and child
alone hug the night.

Embden Pond

As I sat on a pier
Silently kissing a mirror pond,
Waves hushed a banked stillness.
Beyond acres of water
Sailed a two-passenger boat
Through dark tree shadows
Roaring toward the mountain
Leaving behind a world, so new.

Cat

___

Among animals
and humans
I love the cat black
in a lap
on a cold
day
lying
still
eyes closed
to crackling fire
and golden flames
free.

Pure Light

In the evening were the glowing
moon and shining stars, a gift
moving the world. Brighter
now, rays of light,
glimmer of hope; unborn child
on a donkey sleeping in darkness.
We were falling in
Eden, Virgin Mother.
We were waiting on edge
for a new world, for centuries:
praying for you to give birth to
new love and pure light.

The Country Preacher's Folk Prayer

Eternal God,
We come this mornin'
with bowed heads and humble hearts.

Uh hum.

We thank you for sparing us another day
by letting your angels watch over our
bedside while we slumbered and slept.

Uh hum.

We come to you without any form or fashion:
just as we are without one plea.

Uh hum.

You blessed us when we didn't deserve it.
When we traveled down the road of sin,
you snatched us, and made us taste of the
blood of Thy Lamb.

Yes, Lord!

This mornin', touch every human heart.
Transform tears into Heavenly showers
for the salvation of sinful souls.

Yassir.

Remember the sick, the afflicted,
the heavy laden.
Open the windows of Thy Heavenly home.
Let perpetual light shine on them in the
midnight hour.

Yes, Lord.

When we have done all that we can do down here,
take us into Thy Kingdom, where the sun never sets,
where there's no more bigotry, hypocrisy, backbiting;
no more weeping and wailing, before Thy throne, where
you will wipe away our tears; where we can see our
mothers;

Ma Ma!

Where, in that city, where the streets are paved in gold and
adorned with every jewel,
where we can see Jesus, sitting on the throne
of glory.

Ummmm mmmmmm a hummmmmmm

When we get home, when we get home,
when we get home,

we'll rest in Thy bosom
and praise you forever.

Amen

The Anniversary

At church
she'd bow to guest preachers
listening
to their hellfire sermons
her wig resting like graveyard grass
the preacher her half sat near her
in tails like a statue
in a cemetery.

And celebrating his anniversary
he'd dream of silver watching it
rovingly, rovingly
as members dropped it in plates
on Jesus's table.
His heart wild with greed
his money, his church, his anniversary
these belonged to others as well.

Special seats establishing his hierarchy
he'd listen for hours
to hoarse voices singing
to praises for peasants
exalting him and her.

Grinning in the light
and quiet
he'd preach next Sunday
the powerful word
the Bible
tight in his fist.

Morning After Morning

This is after darkness leaves,
It is when birds sing happily,

When the cool breeze kisses clouds
And morning rain makes love to earth.

All are asleep still,
The cat tiptoes around the house.

There is silence here again,
Morning after morning.

It happens repeatedly,
This celebration of peace,

This reaffirmation of love.

The Countryside of Northampton

I will dress now and travel home,
And a new house rest, of bricks and stone made:
One room I will need there, a corner for poetry,
And sit alone at the oak desk.

And I will hug Mom and Dad,
Their steps in concert with canes now,
Home's a feeling and evening a grace here,
And the kitchen warm with bread.

I will go where owls and crickets serenade,
And remember the yellow roses by the fields;
While I drive through mountains, or cities,
I hear my voice echoing a past connecting the now.

Elegy for Therman B. O'Daniel

I remember his voice, rich and golden;
And his urbane manner, majestic as a king;
And how, once meeting, a smile leaped for us,
And he thundered beliefs about journals and words
And how they last.
We sang, too, his melodies
And dreamed,
Our leafs turning to poems and stories;
Our songs tremble their criticism now.

He kindled an eternal flame
That burns hearts, young and old,
And sacrificed twilight years for stars,
And enjoyed the sunrise and sunsets.

If only we could assure him now
That his work reaped harvests for all seasons,
The fruits of his labors save the world.

Forgiveness

Memories linger, beautiful as the moon,
Beautiful that his lying did not destroy my soul,
    and repeatedly, this terrible world;
For my adversary's son is dead, a boy young and divine,
I look at him in his white casket—I turn around
Bend down and hug lightly his father
       with my shoulder catching his tears,
His crying aloud begging God for salvation.

Other Books of Poetry
by Leonard A. Slade, Jr.

────────────